23.70

PEOPLE AT
THE CENTER OF

THE RENAISSANCE

By GAIL B. STEWART

BLACKBIRCH PRESS

An imprint of Thomson Gale, a part of The Thomson Corporation

THOMSON

GALE

Detroit • New York • San Francisco • San Diego • New Haven, Conn.
Waterville, Maine • London • Munich

LIBRARY OF CONGRESS CATALOGING-IN-PUBLICATION DATA

Stewart, Gail B., 1949–
 The Renaissance / by Gail B. Stewart.
   p. cm. — (People at the center of)
Summary: Profiles prominent artists, scientists, explorers, and other innovators of the Renaissance.
 Includes bibliographical references and index.
 ISBN 1-56711-922-0 (hard cover : alk. paper) 1. Renaissance—Biography—Juvenile literature. 2. Europe—Biography—Juvenile literature. I. Title. II. Series.

CB361.S69 2005
920.04'09'024—dc22   2005018440

Printed in the United States of America

⊚ CONTENTS

THE
RENAISSANCE

The Renaissance was a period marked by a revival of interest in the classical arts and literature of ancient Greece and Rome. This revival resulted in one of the greatest cultural movements in history. The Renaissance began in Italy in the early 14th century and continued into the 17th century. During that time, the Renaissance spread north from Italy to France, Germany, England, the Netherlands, and other European countries.

During the Renaissance, an explosion of intellectual energy resulted in accomplishments in painting, sculpture, and literature, along with new ways of thinking about politics and science. There was great interest in discussing humankind's place in the world and people's relationship to God. The Renaissance also resulted in the expansion of physical boundaries, as explorers discovered lands and sea routes they had never dreamed of before.

The atmosphere of energy and creativity during the Renaissance was in direct contrast with conditions in the era that preceded it, known as the Middle Ages. The Middle Ages began in the 5th century A.D., when Germanic tribes

Opposite: Renaissance artists depicted ordinary people realistically, as shown in this self-portrait by Sofonisba Anguissola. Above: Sea exploration during the Renaissance revealed lands and routes previously unknown to Europeans.

The painter Raphael (center) was one of the leading artists of the Renaissance.

overran and brought about the fall of the Roman Empire. Many of the empire's cities fell into ruin, its beautiful buildings and temples were destroyed, and many of its cultural treasures were lost or ruined.

Afterward, Europe gradually became a feudalistic society. Peasants, or common people, were bound as serfs to work the land for members of the nobility. In exchange for their labor, the peasants received the protection of the nobles but very little else. Peasants received no pay for their work, nor did they have hopes for a better life for their children, who were not even permitted to have schooling. Education during the Middle Ages was a luxury reserved only for the nobility—and even that education was limited. Scholars during the Middle Ages believed that religion was the only topic worth studying. The thinking of the day was that people's responsibility on Earth was to serve God so that after they died they could go to heaven.

These attitudes were reflected in the arts of the Middle Ages. The Catholic Church, which was extremely powerful, believed that art and literature should exist only to serve God. Thus, art and poetry almost always dealt with religious themes—either praising God or warning sinners of the punishments of hell. Because the religious message of a work was more important than the art itself, artistic techniques were crude. Paintings, for example, were often dark, and the people depicted in them looked stiff and lifeless.

As Renaissance artists rediscovered classic art, however, they saw that religious themes were not the only themes worth expressing. Renaissance painters such as Raphael and Leonardo da Vinci used perspective, color, and light to bring life to their subjects, which were sometimes regular people rather than religious figures.

The Renaissance was marked by a reawakening of interest in the art and literature of ancient Greece and Rome. The celebration shown here was held to honor the ancient Greek philosopher Plato.

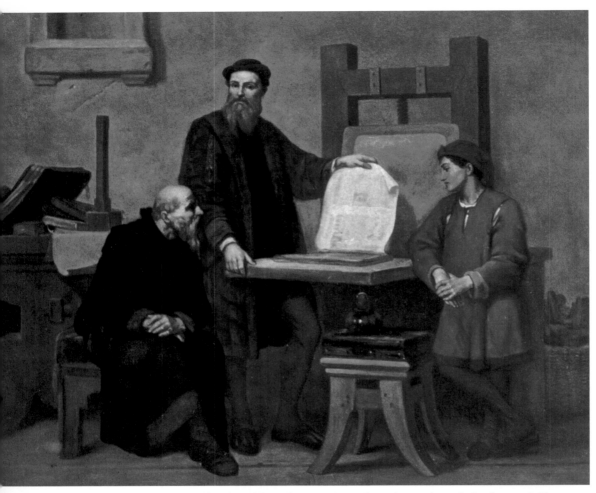

The printing process developed by Johannes Gutenberg (center) made books available to more Europeans than ever before.

The people portrayed in their work were amazingly lifelike and three dimensional, rather than flat and unrealistic.

Literature also changed during the Renaissance. Instead of churning out religious texts as their predecessors had done, writers began to explore classical styles of poetry and prose. One of the first Renaissance writers was a classical scholar named Petrarch. He wrote love poems to a woman named Laura. His poetry popularized the idea of writing about romantic love and the fourteen-line form he used, called a sonnet.

The rebirth of classical thinking led to a new philosophy called humanism. Humanism did not go along with the church's long-held views that minimized the worth of individuals. Humanist philosophers and classical scholars such as Desiderius Erasmus revived the celebration of human accomplishments and ideas and urged the church to encourage freedom of thought and curiosity. Erasmus and other Renaissance thinkers believed that human problems could be solved by such unrestrained ideas.

The burst of energy that resulted in such advances in art, literature, and philosophy led to a surge of new technology as well. One example is Johannes Gutenberg's printing process that involved movable type. It made books—and the ideas they contained—available to more people.

While the Renaissance primarily embraced classical ideas, the quest for new knowledge led some individuals to discover flaws in ancient Roman and Greek thinking. Andreas Vesalius, a brilliant surgeon, dared to contradict the anatomy teachings of Galen, a doctor of ancient Greece. Italian scientist Galileo Galelei disputed Aristotle's teaching that the Sun and the planets revolve around Earth.

This expansion of knowledge beyond the classical thinking of ancient Greece and Rome, as well as the accomplishments in arts, philosophy, and technology that took place during the Renaissance, opened the door to the modern age. The cultural revolution that started in the 14th century and continued for 300 years is still evident today. It is seen not only in Michelangelo's sculptures and Raphael's paintings, but in the daring of today's thinkers as they, too, push the boundaries of what is known into the unknown.

Marco Polo wars born in 1254 into a noble family in Venice, Italy. Just before he was born, his father, Niccolo, and uncle, Maffeo, left Venice on a trading mission to east Asia. By the time the two men returned, Marco was fifteen years old and eager to go with them on their next expedition.

In 1271 Marco, along with Niccolo and Maffeo, sailed from Venice to Palestine. From there they traveled by camel and on foot. They visited Turkey and Persia (present-day Iran) and finally crossed the Gobi Desert. More than three years after leaving Venice, the three travelers arrived at the palace of Kublai Khan, the emperor of Mongolia.

Polo became a great favorite of the khan, as the emperor was known. The young man was skilled at learning languages and quickly made himself at home in Chinese culture. For three years he served the khan as governor of the city of Yangzhou. During that time, Polo visited parts of what are now Vietnam and Thailand.

In 1295 the three Polos returned to Venice. They brought gifts from the khan, including ivory, jade, silk, and a dazzling collection of jewels. Marco wrote a book entitled *Description of the World* about his adventures. At first readers did not believe his stories were true, for many of the things he described—such as paper money, printing, and coal—were still unknown in Europe. Eventually, however, people became excited about the faraway world of China. Polo's book inspired a number of Europeans to visit Asia and learn about the inventions he had seen. It demonstrated to Europeans that there was an important part of the world beyond Europe.

Polo eventually married and had children. He did not return to China, but he worked in Venice as a merchant. He died there in 1324.

Opposite: Through his travels and writings, Marco Polo introduced Europeans to China. Above: This painting depicts Marco Polo kneeling before the khan, or emperor, of Mongolia.

DANTE ALIGHIERI

WROTE IN THE LANGUAGE OF THE PEOPLE

Dante Alighieri, who is usually known only by his first name, was born in Florence, Italy, in 1265. Unlike most young people at that time, Dante received an education in classic Roman and Greek literature as well as religious training. As a college student, he studied in the Italian cities of Padua and Bologna.

Dante was active in politics as a young man. The party he supported in Florence suddenly fell out of favor in the 1290s, however. In 1302 he and other prominent party members were stripped of their possessions and banished from the city. Dante remained in Italy, but he never returned to Florence.

Opposite: Exiled from his native Florence in 1302, Dante Alighieri went on to become one of Italy's most revered poets. Above: The Divine Comedy, *Dante's most famous work, is considered one of the greatest poems ever written.*

While in exile, Dante began to write. One of his first works was an essay in which he argued that literature could be written in the vernacular, or everyday language. Traditionally, such works were written in Latin, which was familiar mainly to scholars, scientists, and writers. Dante believed that using the vernacular —whether Italian, English, or French—could make literature more accessible to common people.

Following his own advice, Dante wrote poetry and essays in Italian on a wide variety of subjects. His most famous work was *La Divina Commedia* (*The Divine Comedy*), a long epic poem about life after death, which he began in 1307 and finished in 1321. Dante himself was the central character. Besides using strong religious themes in the work, he also paid homage to ancient Roman literature by including the Roman poet Virgil as an important character.

The poem stands as one of the greatest epic poems ever written and the first major work not written in Latin. Dante broke new ground by using an innovative verse form that was lyrical with a strong rhythm. The popularity of *The Divine Comedy* was so great that when German inventor Johannes Gutenberg's movable type press made it possible to produce many books, Dante's poem was one of the first literary works to be printed.

Dante died on September 14, 1321, shortly after finishing the last section of his epic. The final section was published after his death.

FRANCESCO PETRARCH

Francesco Petrarch was born in Arezzo, Italy, on July 20, 1304. His father was active in politics and angered some government officials. As a result, the family fled to France, where young Francesco began his education. Almost from the beginning, he loved the poetry and essays of classical Greek and Roman writers. Although he was taking university classes in law, Petrarch abandoned all thoughts of being a lawyer in 1326 and decided to become a poet instead.

One of his inspirations was a woman named Laura, whom he claimed he observed and fell in love with during church services one day. For the rest of his life, Petrarch wrote poetry about her. In 1336 he collected those poems in a book. Petrarch became widely known, and he received invitations to be named poet laureate of both Rome and Paris. He chose the offer from Rome. In a special ceremony in 1341, he was crowned with a laurel wreath, as poet laureates were in ancient Rome.

Petrarch continued to write poetry, most of it in Latin. He wrote a long epic poem about the great history of ancient Rome, and he wrote a number of religious poems, too. He wrote a great deal of his love poetry in a centuries-old form called the Italian sonnet. His use of the sonnet and the Latin language resulted in a revival of interest in the classic literature of ancient Rome. This interest was a hallmark of the Renaissance.

In his later years, Petrarch suffered from fevers and fainting spells. His friends urged him to stop writing and to rest, but he insisted that a pen weighed nothing. The thought that his writing could give other people pleasure made him happy. He died on July 19, 1374, at his writing desk.

Opposite: Francesco Petrarch was crowned with a laurel wreath to signify his status as poet laureate of Rome. Above: Petrarch's sonnets were inspired by his love for a woman named Laura.

DEVELOPED A WAY TO PRINT

Johannes Gutenberg was born on February 23, 1395, in Mainz, Germany. Very little is known about his early life, other than that he came from a wealthy family. Gutenberg enjoyed tinkering with mechanical things and wanted to become an inventor.

Printing fascinated Gutenberg. In the 15th century there were few books printed in Europe, and those that existed were religious texts. Monks wrote these texts out by hand using quill pens. Copying a single manuscript could take years. Other written material, such as posters, were printed by carving patterns on wooden blocks. The blocks were covered in ink and then paper was pressed on them to create an image. To print a book this way would have been virtually impossible, because each page would have to be hand carved onto a wooden block.

Opposite: Johannes Gutenberg revolutionized the printing process. Above: This painting depicts Gutenberg in his workshop.

Gutenberg began to experiment with the idea of a printing press that used movable type: individual letters and punctuation marks cast in metal. The individual letters could be arranged into sentences. After a page was printed, the letters could be separated and reused to create the next page.

Gutenberg placed a tray containing the rows of type on one part of a press. On the other part he put a large wooden block that would press the paper to the type. He used soft leather balls filled with wool to ink the type. After placing a piece of paper between the block and the type, he turned a wooden screw that lowered the block onto the paper. The pressure transferred the ink to the paper.

The first book Gutenberg and his assistants printed was the *Bible*. It took five years to print 210 copies, because every step was done by hand and each book contained 1,280 pages. The project was a success. Within a few years, hundreds of printing shops throughout Europe were using Gutenberg's movable type idea. By 1470 more than 4,000 books were being printed each year. This was one of the greatest accomplishments of the Renaissance, for it made books on a variety of interesting topics widely available to the public for the first time.

Gutenberg was honored by being named a member of the royal court of Germany. He died in Mainz on February 3, 1468.

LEONARDO DA VINCI

RENAISSANCE MAN

Leonardo da Vinci was born on April 15, 1452, in Vinci, a mountain town in central Italy. As a boy, Leonardo was interested in drawing animals and plants and in creating pictures of ideas he had for inventions. His father noticed Leonardo's artistic talent, and when the boy was fourteen, arranged for him to become an apprentice to a famous sculptor and painter named Andrea del Verrocchio.

As an apprentice, Leonardo studied the basic techniques of sculpture and painting. Verrocchio was impressed with Leonardo's work and allowed the boy to collaborate with him on one of his paintings, *The Baptism of Christ*. Leonardo was allowed to paint one of the two angels pictured, and a legend says that when Verrocchio saw how much more lifelike Leonardo's angel was than his own, he vowed never to paint again.

Leonardo continued to work on his own, in a studio in the city of Florence. In each of his paintings, he showed an attention to detail that made the people in his paintings look amazingly realistic. His most famous paintings were *The Last Supper*, completed in 1493, and the *Mona Lisa*, completed in 1505.

Leonardo was famous for more than his paintings, however. In fact, his contributions to the times came in such a variety of areas that he is often referred to

Opposite: Artist, inventor, and scientist Leonardo da Vinci was one of the greatest thinkers of the Renaissance. Above: Leonardo finished his masterpiece, the Mona Lisa, in 1505.

One of Leonardo's most famous paintings, The Last Supper, *shows Jesus breaking bread with his twelve disciples.*

as "the Renaissance Man." He was keenly interested in science and did a number of studies of the human body. He was one of the first to create accurate scientific drawings of bones and muscles. He also made intricate drawings of ideas he had for a parachute, a flying machine, a movable bridge, and hundreds of other inventions.

Leonardo spent most of his life in Italy, but in 1517 he was invited to come to France. The French king, Francis I, gave Leonardo the title of "Master of All Arts and Sciences" and offered him a lavish home and studio where he could work. He died there in 1519.

Lorenzo de Medici was born on January 1, 1449, in Florence, Italy. He was extremely bright, and because his family was very wealthy, he was tutored by some of the best teachers in Italy. His favorite subjects were reading and creative writing. By the age of fourteen, Medici was writing exceptional poetry.

The Medici family was the most powerful in Florence, and Lorenzo reaped the benefits of his family name when his grandfather, Cosimo de Medici, died in 1464. The young Medici began a political career and was elected to several councils in the city, including the most famous, the Council of One Hundred. It was made up of the most influential men in Florence.

Medici was young, but he had been schooled in the use of political power since childhood. He gradually was given more authority by other Florentine leaders. He controlled Florence's banking industry and fought off an attempt by another wealthy family to overthrow his family's empire.

It is not because of his political power that Medici became famous, however. His advocacy on behalf of Florence's art community is what gained him lasting fame. Like his grandfather before him, Medici was a great supporter of the arts. Cosimo had given a great deal of money to establish the first public library in the city, and the beautiful structure was filled with original Greek and Roman manuscripts. Lorenzo soon became famous for even greater generosity. He spent the modern equivalent of $6 million on additional books for the library. He also supported the humanism movement by reestablishing the University of Pisa, where students from all over the world could learn about the ideas of classical scholars.

His love of the arts, combined with his immense family wealth, made Medici the most important patron of art during the Renaissance. He encouraged the young sculptor Michelangelo and helped him meet other artists, scholars, and writers in Florence. Medici also commissioned many sculptures and other works of art by the talented artist.

Medici spent the last year of his life working on plans for projects to beautify Florence. He had suffered from poor health for years, and on April 8, 1492, he died.

His family's vast wealth allowed Lorenzo de Medici to sponsor artists and cultural projects. He supported the first public library in Florence, Italy, and was a patron of the artist Michelangelo, among others.

DESIDERIUS ERASMUS

PRINCE OF THE HUMANISTS

Desiderius Erasmus was born in Rotterdam, in the Netherlands, in about 1466. He went to a religious school and was an excellent student. He studied to become a priest and was ordained in 1492. He was eventually sent to Paris to study *Bible* history. He found his classes dull, however, and preferred reading on his own—especially classical literature by ancient Greek and Roman authors.

In 1499 Erasmus visited England, where he was introduced to Sir Thomas More, a humanist scholar. Humanism was an important intellectual movement that grew out of the Renaissance. The movement's ideas contrasted with those of the Catholic Church. Since the Middle Ages, the church's main focus had been saving souls. Education was seen only as a means to that end. Humanists, however, believed that people and their achievements were vitally important. They stressed that education and exposure to the classical art and literature of ancient Greece and Rome were more important than the church's mission of saving people's souls. Educated individuals could contribute by helping solve society's problems and thereby create a more beautiful world.

Opposite: Desiderius Erasmus's translation of the New Testament *corrected errors and omissions in earlier editions. Above: Erasmus encouraged the teaching of classical Greek and Roman works.*

Erasmus was excited by the ideas of humanism. He began to write letters to other scholars of the time, urging them to work toward the education of students by studying classical Greek and Roman writers. While he supported the work of his humanist colleagues who were teaching classic literature and philosophy, however, Erasmus focused most of his efforts in a different direction.

Erasmus had discovered original Greek manuscripts of the *Bible's New Testament*, and realized that some of the original meaning of the *Bible* had been lost in translation through the centuries. Erasmus created a new translation of these ancient writings, which were published in 1516. This allowed people to read the *New Testament* in its entirety, without errors and omissions.

Erasmus moved back to Holland in his later life and died there in 1536.

Christopher Columbus was born in Genoa, Italy, in the fall of 1451. His family manufactured woolen products. Columbus was not interested in joining the family business. Instead he yearned to be a sailor. At the age of fourteen, he joined a ship's crew and went to sea for the first time.

As he became skilled at sailing, Columbus studied navigation, astronomy, and map making. His journeys grew longer and took him from Iceland to Benin, a country on the west coast of Africa. After returning from Benin, Columbus began to plan an even greater expedition.

At that time, many European countries sought to find a water route to what they called the Indies—India, China, and Japan. The Portuguese intended to get to the Indies by sailing around the tip of Africa. Columbus, however, thought it might be easier to sail to the Indies by going west, across the Atlantic.

He persuaded King Ferdinand and Queen Isabella of Spain to finance the expedition, and on August 3, 1492, his three ships set sail from Palos, Spain. Members of his crew became concerned as the weeks went by with no sighting of land. Finally, on October 12, Columbus and his men saw the white cliffs of a small island in the Bahamas, which they mistakenly assumed was part of the Indies. He went on to reach the islands of Cuba and Hispaniola. Columbus believed he had arrived in the Indies, and called the native people he encountered "Indians." He returned to Spain, bringing some of these people as slaves for the king and queen.

Ferdinand and Isabella were overjoyed at Columbus's discovery and gave him the title of "Admiral of the Ocean," which was the highest honor a sea captain could attain. Columbus told them that he had seen lands where there was an abundance of gold. The king and queen ordered him to return to the Indies. They wanted him to bring back treasure and to establish Spanish colonies there.

Columbus made three more voyages to the New World and set foot on the shore of Venezuela and parts of Central America. He never realized, however, that the lands he had discovered were not part of Asia. Even so, Columbus's expeditions were extraordinarily valuable, for they opened the Atlantic as a route for sea voyages. His exploration also paved the way for contact between Europe and the Americas. He died in 1506, shortly after his last voyage.

Italian explorer Christopher Columbus set out to find a water route from Europe to Asia in 1492. He failed to do so, but his voyages led to the European conquest of the New World in the sixteenth century.

VASCO DA GAMA

FOUND A ROUTE TO INDIA

Vasco da Gama was born around 1460, at the seaport of Sines, in western Portugal. From the time he was very young, da Gama was interested in ships and sailing, and he hoped to be a sea captain when he grew up. In school he learned as much as he could about navigation, astronomy, mathematics, and other subjects that could help him achieve this goal.

In 1492 da Gama realized his dream when he became a commander on ships that patrolled the coast of Portugal. Five years later, King Manuel I of Portugal requested a more important mission of da Gama—to find a sea route from Portugal to India. India was a highly sought-after trading partner because of the jewels, gold, spices, and beautiful fabrics produced there. Becoming the first European country to enter a trade agreement with India would be enormously profitable. A sea route to India had not yet been found, however.

Da Gama was excited about the assignment, and on July 8, 1497, he set sail as the commander of 4 ships and 170 men. They rounded the tip of Africa, known as the Cape of Good Hope, and headed north to trading ports in what are now the nations of Mozambique and Kenya. As he neared India, da Gama and his crew had difficulties with Arab traders, who resented European interference in India and tried to seize da Gama's ships. He finally reached Calicut, India, on May 20, 1498, and returned to Portugal the following year.

Opposite: In 1497, Vasco da Gama opened a vital water route from Europe to Asia. Above: Upon his return home to Portugal, da Gama was honored by King Manuel I.

Although only 50 of his original crew survived illness and skirmishes with hostile Arab traders, da Gama was praised for his achievement. Just as Columbus pushed the boundaries of the known world to the west, da Gama's exploration had opened a door to India. Da Gama made a return voyage to India in 1502 and was appointed as the king's representative there. He died on December 24, 1524.

Michelangelo Buonarroti, known for most of his life simply as Michelangelo, was born on March 6, 1475, in a little town near Florence, Italy. He did not enjoy school and often sneaked away to draw or paint. He also loved to walk around the city and view public sculptures and paintings.

Michelangelo left school at the age of twelve to become an apprentice to two famous artists, the Ghirlandajo brothers. He left before his apprenticeship was over, however, for he felt he had learned all he could from them. He found that he was far more interested in sculpture than in painting. At the age of sixteen he went to a special school for young artists sponsored by the wealthy art patron Lorenzo de Medici.

Medici took an interest in Michelangelo's art, and commissioned him to do work for the Medici palace. He also introduced Michelangelo to other wealthy citizens, who were willing to pay him to create sculptures for their homes. During this time, Michelangelo visited a local hospital, where doctors permitted him to study the muscles and bones of corpses that were awaiting burial. This study helped him make his sculptures far more lifelike than the work of other artists.

In 1497 Michelangelo was invited to Rome, where the pope asked him to create a statue that would be displayed in the Basilica of St. Peter. After two years, Michelangelo presented what many believe is his masterpiece—the *Pietà*, a marble sculpture of Mary holding Jesus's body after the crucifixion. From that point on, Michelangelo was considered the finest sculptor of the Renaissance, not only because of the lifelike look of his work but because of the textures and fine detail he could create from marble.

Although Michelangelo was primarily a sculptor, his most famous work is a painting that is roughly the size of two and a half tennis courts. In 1508, Pope Julius II asked Michelangelo to paint the huge ceiling of the Sistine Chapel in the Vatican. For three years he worked, suspended 60 feet (18m) in the air from the ceiling, lying on his back as he painted. The ceiling was completed in 1511 and depicts various scenes from *Old Testament* stories, as well as prophets and other notable figures. It is considered one of the wonders of the world.

Michelangelo continued painting and sculpting throughout his life. He died in Rome at the age of 89 on February 18, 1564.

Michelangelo is recognized as one of the greatest artists of all time. Originally a sculptor, he turned to painting at the request of Pope Julius II, who commissioned him to paint the ceiling of the Sistine Chapel.

MARTIN LUTHER

CALLED FOR CHURCH REFORMS

Martin Luther was born in Eisleben in what is now Germany on November 10, 1483. His parents were very religious but had no formal education. They both saw, however, that their son was very bright and encouraged him to study. He went to college and studied law. Later Luther decided to become a priest. He was ordained in 1507, and he taught theology at the University of Wittenberg in Germany.

Although Luther found his religious career interesting, he became increasingly frustrated and alarmed at the corruption he saw in the Catholic Church. He especially opposed the selling of indulgences, or official pardons from sins. Luther believed that indulgences were wrong and that priests who sold them made it easy for wealthy people to continue to commit sins.

On October 31, 1517, Luther made his disgust public. He wrote a list of 95 reasons why indulgences were wrong. He nailed the list to the door of the church in Wittenberg. Called the "Ninety-Five Theses," this document infuriated church officials.

Luther continued finding fault with the church. He felt that only God could forgive sins, not the pope. He also believed that the pope was not infallible, as the church taught. In 1521 Luther was excommunicated, or expelled, from the Catholic Church. Although he was considered an enemy by church officials, many Christians agreed with Luther.

Luther's actions launched a movement called the Reformation, which resulted in Protestantism. From that time on, there was no longer one Christian church in Europe. By 1550 a number of other churches, including one bearing Luther's name, had been formed. Each was a little different from the next. Luther continued teaching at the University of Wittenberg until his death on February 18, 1546.

Opposite: Disgusted with the corruption he saw in the Catholic Church, Martin Luther called for reform. Above: Luther posted his "Ninety-Five Theses" on the door of the church in Wittenberg, Germany, in 1517.

RAPHAEL SANZIO

GLORIFIED THE RENAISSANCE SPIRIT

Raphael Sanzio was born in Urbino, Italy, in 1483. His father was a painter and recognized the talent of his young son. At age eleven, Raphael was sent to work as an apprentice to a painter named Perugino. Under Perugino's discipline, Raphael learned the use of color, light, and perspective, or the technique of making objects appear three dimensional on a flat canvas.

Opposite: A master of perspective, painter Raphael Sanzio was long considered the greatest painter in history. Above: This painting shows Raphael at work on a portrait of a woman.

In 1504 Raphael (he then used only his first name) moved to Florence. There he studied the paintings of Leonardo da Vinci and Michelangelo—both of whom had spent a great deal of time in that city. The paintings Raphael created during this time show the influence of those artists.

In 1508 Pope Julius II, eager for Rome to be restored to its ancient grandeur, asked Raphael to come to Rome as part of a group of highly skilled artists and architects. He created a large number of paintings and frescoes (paintings done on plaster) that decorated a number of churches and even the walls of the Pope's living quarters in the Vatican. One of the most famous was *The School of Athens*, which showed two great Greek philosophers, Plato and Aristotle.

Raphael's art was wildly popular. He created many paintings that glorified the spirit of the Renaissance—the new appreciation of ancient Rome and Greece. He was working in Rome in 1520 when he became ill and died at the age of 37. For more than two centuries, he was considered the greatest painter in history.

Andreas Vesalius was born on December 31, 1514, in Brussels, in what is now the country of Belgium. He was interested in biology and chemistry and studied to become a doctor. When he was 23, he became a professor of anatomy at the University of Padua in Italy, the most widely respected medical school in Europe at the time.

For many years the Catholic Church had forbidden the dissection of dead bodies, so most doctors learned about anatomy by studying the bodies of dead animals. Shortly before Vesalius became a doctor, the church relaxed its rules and allowed medical students to study the bodies of hanged criminals. Vesalius took advantage of the opportunity and made careful notes and diagrams of the things he saw in his dissections.

Instruction in medical schools at that time was based on the teachings of the ancient Greek physician Galen, who died in A.D. 199. Galen's work was based on animal dissections, however. From his own experiments on human corpses, Vesalius observed that much of what he had learned as a young medical student was incorrect. The heart was not in the center of the chest, as he had been taught, but rather just to the left of center. There were no bones in the heart, as many believed.

Vesalius began teaching in a different way. He brought cadavers into his lecture hall and dissected them while his classes looked on. It is said that he attracted such large crowds for his dissections that one large hall began to collapse.

In 1543 Vesalius published his drawings and notes in a book called *Fabrica*, or *The Structure of the Human Body*. It was illustrated with more than 270 detailed woodcuts showing close-up views of muscles, bones, and internal organs. The book was a landmark, for it contained information that for the first time was based on observation of actual human bodies. It was also extremely controversial because Vesalius had dared to contradict Galen's work.

Although he had furthered the study of anatomy with his revolutionary work, Vesalius was condemned by older physicians schooled in Galen's teachings. He was forced to burn his remaining notes. He died in a shipwreck after a trip to Palestine in 1564.

Physician Andreas Vesalius used his observations of corpses to record accurate information about the structure of the human body.

GERARDUS MERCATOR

Gerardus Mercator was born on March 5, 1512, in Rupelmonde, Flanders, near present-day Antwerp, Belgium. His parents died when he was very young, and he was raised by an uncle, who insisted the boy get a good education. Mercator studied a variety of subjects, including astronomy, philosophy, and geography.

When he finished college, Mercator set up a workshop where he made globes, navigation instruments, and sundials. His passion, however, was making maps. At first, he created detailed maps of Louvain, the city in which he lived, and of other places in Flanders. Mercator's maps were important, for they were not merely copies of maps already in use. Instead they were based on his own surveys and measurements. In 1554 he made a map of Europe in which he corrected errors from previous maps. After studying the logs of navigators and sea captains, Mercator found that current maps showed the Mediterranean Sea too long by ten degrees of longitude. In addition, the Black and Baltic seas were depicted incorrectly. His corrections made the Mercator map the most accurate one in existence in the 1500s.

Opposite: Gerardus Mercator developed a revolutionary mapmaking method that improved navigation. Above: Mercator found a way to depict the round Earth on a flat map.

Another of Mercator's innovations was his world map, completed in 1569. He represented the round Earth on a flat map in a new way. This method, which became known as the Mercator projection, had the lines of longitude and the lines of latitude appear as straight lines that crossed at right angles. By drawing these lines straight, Mercator made the map easy for a sailor or other navigator to use in charting unfamiliar territory. If two locations were known and plotted on Mercator's map, a navigator could connect them with a straight line and find the compass direction that would take him from one place to the other. Mercator's map provided travelers with a more accurate system of exploring the world during the Renaissance and for centuries afterward.

Mercator spent the last years of his life creating the first book of maps, which he named an atlas. Some of the maps were drawn by Mercator; others were drawn by his son and grandsons. Mercator's atlas was published in 1595, a year after his death.

CHALLENGED CLASSIC SCIENCE

Galileo Galilei was born in Pisa, Italy, on Feburary 15, 1564. He enjoyed science as a young student and decided to study mathematics as well as physical science. He became a professor of mathematics at the University of Padua in 1592.

Galileo felt it was necessary for scientists to observe and experiment, rather than to blindly follow beliefs that had never been proven. Almost all the physical science in Galileo's time was based on 2,000-year-old theories passed down from Aristotle and other ancient Greek thinkers. Although the Renaissance witnessed a rebirth of interest in the classic thinkers, Galileo did not intend to accept their ideas without proof.

One of these ideas was that when two objects were dropped from the same height, the heavier one would fall faster than the lighter one. Galileo disproved this theory when he climbed the leaning tower of Pisa, dropped objects of various weights, and found that they fell at the same rate.

In addition to rethinking ancient theories, Galileo made some spectacular contributions to the study of astronomy and other areas of science. He improved the telescope by inventing a lens that increased its magnification by ten times. With this telescope, he was the first to see and draw the craters of the moon and document the four moons of the planet Jupiter.

Eventually Galileo's inquisitive mind caused him great trouble. One of Aristotle's theories was that the planets and the Sun all revolved around the Earth. A Polish astronomer named Nicolaus Copernicus theorized in the early 1500s that the Earth and its planets actually revolved around the Sun. Galileo found evidence with his telescope that Copernicus had been right. Catholic Church leaders, who had the power to dictate what could be taught, were angry, for the church believed that God had put Earth at the center of the universe. Church leaders banned Galileo's idea and told him to cease his experiments.

Galileo would not stop, however. He continued to support what his experiments showed him. He was convicted of heresy in 1633 and sentenced to life in prison. He died on January 8, 1642.

Using observations he made with his improved telescope, scientist and mathematician Galileo Galilei proved that the Sun, not the Earth, is the center of the solar system.

1274	Marco Polo arrives at the palace of Kublai Khan of Mongolia.
1321	Dante completes *The Divine Comedy*.
1349	Francesco Petrarch writes his first sonnets.
1450	Johannes Gutenberg invents the printing press.
1469	Lorenzo de Medici becomes head of the government of Florence.
1492	Christopher Columbus reaches the Americas.
1498	Vasco da Gama and his crew reach India.
1505	Leonardo da Vinci completes the *Mona Lisa*.
1508	At the request of Pope Julius II, Raphael joins other artists in a project to restore the beauty of Rome.
1511	Michelangelo finishes painting the ceiling of the Sistine Chapel.
1516	Erasmus publishes his translation of the *New Testament*.
1517	Martin Luther writes his "Ninety-Five Theses" against the practice of indulgences by the Catholic Church.
1543	Andreas Vesalius publishes his book on human anatomy.
1595	Gerardus Mercator's atlas is published.
1633	Galileo is convicted of heresy for contradicting Aristotle's theory that the Sun revolves around the Earth.

This painting depicts Christopher Columbus arriving on the island of San Salvador, in what is today the Bahamas, at the end of his first journey in 1492.

FOR FURTHER INFORMATION

BOOKS

James Barter, *A Travel Guide to Renaissance Florence*. San Diego: Lucent, 2003.

Miriam Greenblatt, *Lorenzo de Medici and Renaissance Italy*. New York: Benchmark/Marshall Cavendish, 2003.

Paul F. Grendler, *The Renaissance: An Encyclopedia for Students*. New York: Charles Scribner's Sons, 2004.

Kathryn Hinds, *The Church*. New York: Benchmark, 2004.

Andrew Langley, *Leonardo & His Times*. New York: Dorling Kindersley, 2000.

WEB SITES

The Renaissance
www.learner.org/exhibits/renaissance
This site provides a wealth of information aimed at students—from information on math and science during the fifteenth century to exploration, art, and even a tour of Florence during the Renaissance.

Renaissance Art (Art History on the Web)
www.witcombe.sbc.edu/ARTHLinks2/html
This site contains links to biographies and images of some of the most exciting sculpture, painting, and architecture from the Renaissance.

INDEX

Cover photos: © Kunstsammlungen Dresden/Bridgeman Art Library (main image);

© Bettmann/CORBIS (upper left); © Stefano Bianchetti/CORBIS (upper right)

© Jaime Abecasis/SuperStock, 39

© Archivo Iconografico S.A./CORBIS, 14, 24, 27, 34

The Art Archive/Museo de Arte Antiga Lisbon/Dagli Orti, 28

© Bettmann/CORBIS, 11, 12, 16, 43

Bildarchiv Preussischer Kulturbesitz/Art Resource, NY, 17

Corel Corporation, 19

© Fine Art Photographic Library/CORBIS, 6

Erich Lessing/Art Resource, NY, 7, 15

Mary Evans Picture Library, 4, 8, 25, 29

© Ali Meyer/CORBIS, 5

© Michael Maslan Historic Photographs/CORBIS, 38

North Wind Picture Archives, 33

Portrait of Andrea Vesalius (1514–64) (oil on canvas), Calcar, Jan

Stephen (1499–c. 1546/50)/Hermitage, St. Petersburg,

Russia/Bridgeman Art Library, 36

Scala/Art Resource, NY, 40

Stock Montage/Hulton Archive /Getty Images, 13, 18, 31, 32, 35

© Stock Montage/Superstock, 10

© SuperStock, Inc., 20–21, 23

ABOUT THE AUTHOR

Gail B. Stewart earned an undergraduate degree from Gustavus Adolphus College in St. Peter, Minnesota. She did graduate work in English, linguistics, and curriculum study at the College of St. Thomas and the University of Minnesota. She taught English and reading for more than ten years. She has written more than 90 books for young people, including a series for Lucent Books called The Other America. She has written many books on historical topics such as World War I and the Warsaw ghetto. Stewart and her husband live in Minneapolis with their three sons, Ted, Elliot, and Flynn; two dogs; and a cat. When she is not writing, she enjoys reading, walking, and watching her sons play soccer.